feeling
ill?

Chickenpox

By Jillian Powell

Contents

WHAT'S WRONG?

If you catch chickenpox, you feel unwell for a few days. You may have a runny nose and be sneezing or coughing. You may feel hot and have a headache or stomach ache. After a few days, spots start to appear on your head, face and body.

Did you know?

Chickenpox gets its name from 'cicer' the Latin word for *chick peas*.

Sally's story

I felt unwell and then I saw the spots on my face. They were really itchy. I was a bit worried at first because I didn't know what they were.

CATCHING CHICKENPOX

Chickenpox is a **virus** that you catch from other people. You breathe in tiny drops of the virus in the air or pick them up on your hands. It spreads easily in families and schools.

8

Dear Doc

Mum thinks my sister might have chickenpox. Will I catch it?

It's likely, because you can catch it from someone before the spots appear.

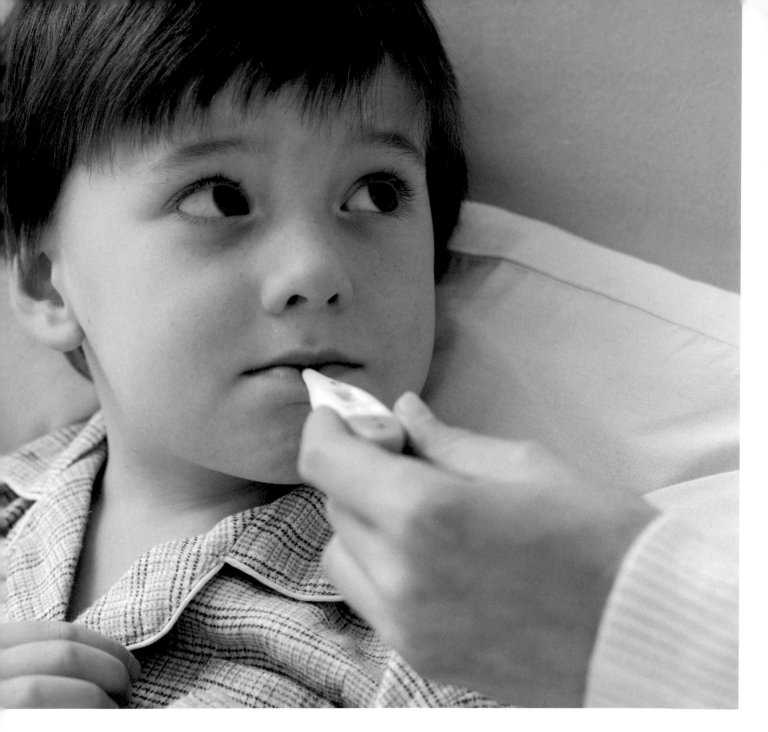

WHAT's GOING ON?

When you catch chickenpox, your body starts making **antibodies** in your blood to fight the virus. Your normal body temperature is 37°C. It goes up when it is fighting a virus. This gives you a **fever** and makes you feel hot and unwell.

Dear Doc

How soon do chickenpox spots appear?

You can have the virus for about 10 - 21 days before the spots appear.

CHICKENPOX RASH

A chickenpox **rash** starts as itchy red spots. They turn into **blisters** that go cloudy, then form scabs. Spots can go on appearing for up to about a week. After that they start to form a **scab**. You can pass the virus on to others until all the scabs are dry.

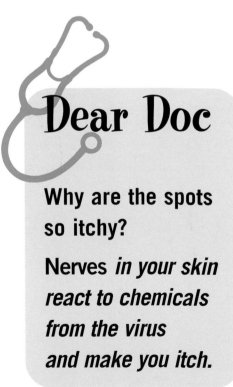

Dear Doc

Why are the spots so itchy?

Nerves *in your skin react to chemicals from the virus and make you itch.*

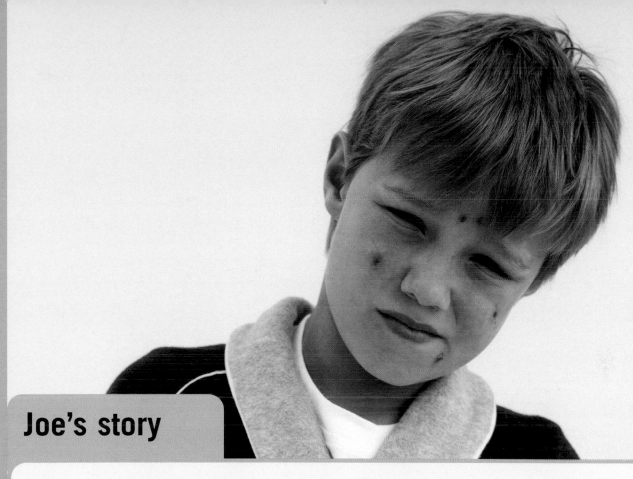

My brother Ollie had chickenpox, then I caught it. We couldn't go on holiday because we could have given it to other people on the plane. We had to play at home instead.

TREATING CHICKENPOX

Chickenpox spots are most itchy in the first few days. You should try not to scratch them as this can spread **germs** under the skin and leave scars. It helps to keep your skin cool. Wear cotton clothes, and take baths with some **oatmeal** or **bicarbonate of soda** in.

14

Dear Doc

I keep scratching my spots whilst I'm asleep. What can I do?

Try wearing some cotton gloves in bed.

Max's story

My spots were really itchy. I couldn't stop scratching them. Mum dabbed some calamine lotion on and it really helped!

GETTING BETTER

You can help to get over chickenpox by resting and drinking plenty of cool drinks. Foods like fruit jellies and ice lollies are easy to eat and will help to soothe your throat. If you have a high temperature, the doctor may give you something to help to bring it down.

Dear Doc

What is the best medicine for chickenpox?

The best medicine is rest, because your body fights germs best when you are sleeping.

Gabriel's story

I had spots in my mouth so I didn't feel like eating much. I had lots of fruit juice and jellies because they were easy to eat.

17

Dear Doc

Can you prevent chickenpox?

In some countries, children can have a vaccination to stop them catching the virus.

AFTER CHICKENPOX

When you have had chickenpox, you almost never catch it again. This is because your body learns to make antibodies that stop the virus becoming active again. Sometimes, it can appear again as a painful rash called **shingles**. This usually happens if your **immune system** becomes weak.

STAYING FIT

Your body has to fight off germs every day. You can keep your immune system strong by eating healthy foods like fresh fruits and vegetables. They contain **vitamin C** which helps you to get better. Exercise keeps you fit and helps you make white blood cells to fight germs.

20

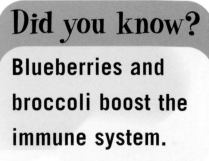

Did you know?

Blueberries and broccoli boost the immune system.

We did a project about fruit at school. We made a table of fruits that contain lots of vitamin C like oranges and kiwis.

21

Glossary

Antibodies	chemicals made in the blood by white blood cells to fight germs
Bicarbonate of soda	a white fizzy powder, sometimes used in baking
Blisters	little bumps on the skin that contain watery fluid
Chick peas	small round peas that are cooked as a vegetable
Fever	a high body temperature due to an illness
Germs	tiny living things that can cause illnesses
Immune system	parts of the body that fight infection
Nerves	special cells that send signals from the body to the brain
Oatmeal	oats that have been rolled or ground
Rash	when the skin becomes bumpy or red, itchy or sore
Scab	a crust that forms on the skin to protect a cut or wound while it heals
Shingles	a painful skin rash that is caused by the chickenpox virus
Vaccination	a skin prick with a needle to protect against an illness
Virus	a germ that causes colds and other illnesses
Vitamin C	a substance found in foods including fruit and vegetables that we need to stay healthy and fight illnesses